All About Awareness

By
Bella Hope Smith

MAPLE
PUBLISHERS

All About Awareness

Author: Bella Hope Smith

Copyright © 2025 Bella Hope Smith

The author asserts the moral right to be identified as the author of this work.

The right of Bella Hope Smith to be identified as author of this work has been asserted by the author in accordance with section 77 and 78 of the Copyright, Designs and Patents Act 1988.

First Published in 2025

ISBN 978-1-83538-712-2 (Paperback)

Cover Design and Book Layout by:
    White Magic Studios
    www.whitemagicstudios.co.uk

Published by:
    Maple Publishers
    Fairbourne Drive, Atterbury,
    Milton Keynes,
    MK10 9RG, UK
    www.maplepublishers.com

A CIP catalogue record for this title is available from the British Library.

All rights reserved. No part of this book may be reproduced or translated in any form or by any means, electronic or mechanical, including photocopying, recording or by any information storage and retrieval system without written permission from the author.

CONTENTS

Introduction 5

Rhyming CPR Poem 6

CPR 7

CPR 8

Suicide 10

Homelessness 12

Motor Neurone Disease 14

Autism 15

Grief 16

Tourette's 18

Body Dysmorphia 19

Cancer 20

Anti-Discrimination 22

Dyspraxia 23

Alcoholism	24
Periods	26
ADHD	27
River Pollution	28
Anti-Knife Crime	30
Dyslexia	31
Animal Cruelty	32
Loneliness	34
Skin Conditions	35
Panic Attacks	36
Domestic Abuse	38
How To Write Your Own Awareness Poems	39
Self Awareness	40
Mighty Mind Mantra's For Men	42
Rejuvenating Rhyming Affirmations	43
Mystical, Spiritual, Poetical	44

All About Awareness

Introduction

Hello everyone, thank you for buying my book. I wanted to write this book, to shine the light on tough and important topics, that need to be talked about and be made aware of.

Each poem that I have written, I wanted to create a hard hitting message to really make these issues stand out, heard and understood. A few of my poems I have written in a thought provoking way, to really get people to think and reflect.

Some of my poems I have written from the perspective of how someone may feel going through hard times, as I have known people that have gone through, or are going through a few of the tough topics that I am writing about in my book.

Writing my poems I want to make others, Aware, Care & Share.

I end each of my poems, on a lighter note or more optimistic view. If you would like to contact me, please email; spirituallypoetical@gmail.com

Bella Hope Smith

Rhyming CPR Poem

I have written a rhyming CPR poem, to let everyone know how to do this important procedure on someone if they need it. I have written it in small steps so it's easier to follow. Below is a picture on how you perform the rescue breaths on someone when doing CPR. At the end of the poem, there is a picture on how to do the correct hand position when doing chest compressions on someone.

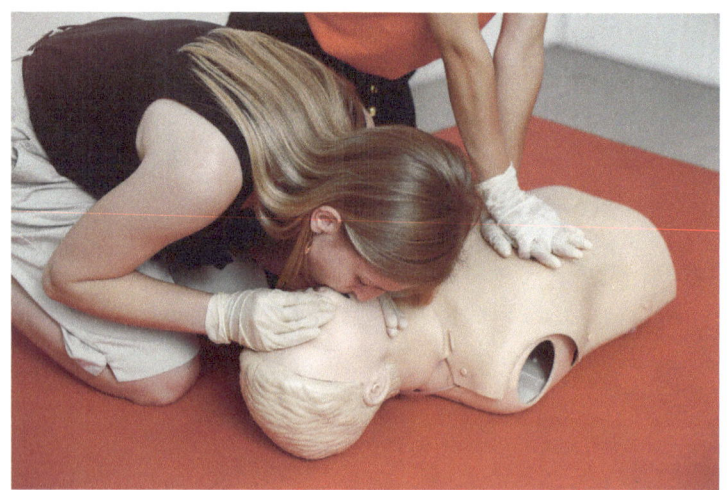

All About Awareness

CPR

CPR stands for Cardiopulmonary Resuscitation. It is vital to do in a life or death situation.

If someone is struggling or collapses in front of you. Phoning the emergency services is the first thing to do.

Check on the person and say loudly "Are you ok?" Whilst gently tapping their shoulders, and seeing if there is a response or sound. If there's no reaction, place the person on their back and shout for help if people are around.

Open the person's airways by gently tilting their head back at a 45 degree angle, and lifting up their chin. This allows the throat to be free of obstructions, making the airways clear so the CPR process can begin.

See if the person is breathing, or if they are gasping for air. A person may have stopped breathing, but a pulse might still be there.

Put your hands on top of each other, with fingers interlocked, keeping elbows locked and arms kept straight. Doing this will get the right compression position, which is what we want to create.

Bella Hope Smith

CPR

Position your hand so the heel of it is in the centre of the person's chest. Push down firmly about 2 inches depth per compression, and keeping a steady continious rhythm is best.

Do 100 to 120 compressions per minute, to help get the blood flowing to the heart. We want the circulation to get round the body, giving the chance for the heart to re-start.

After 30 consecutive compressions, give the person 2 rescue breaths. This is done by pinching their nose shut, sealing your mouth with theirs, and giving them one big breath; allowing the rise and fall of their chest.

After 2 rescue breaths continue with more compressions, or if there is a defibrillator available, you can apply that too. It has all the instructions on how to use it, so you know exactly what to do.

Keep repeating the whole process, whilst you are waiting for the medical teams arrival. Doing CPR on someone, gives them a better chance of survival.

If anyone needs help or collapses, please don't think twice. About doing CPR on them, as you may just save their life.

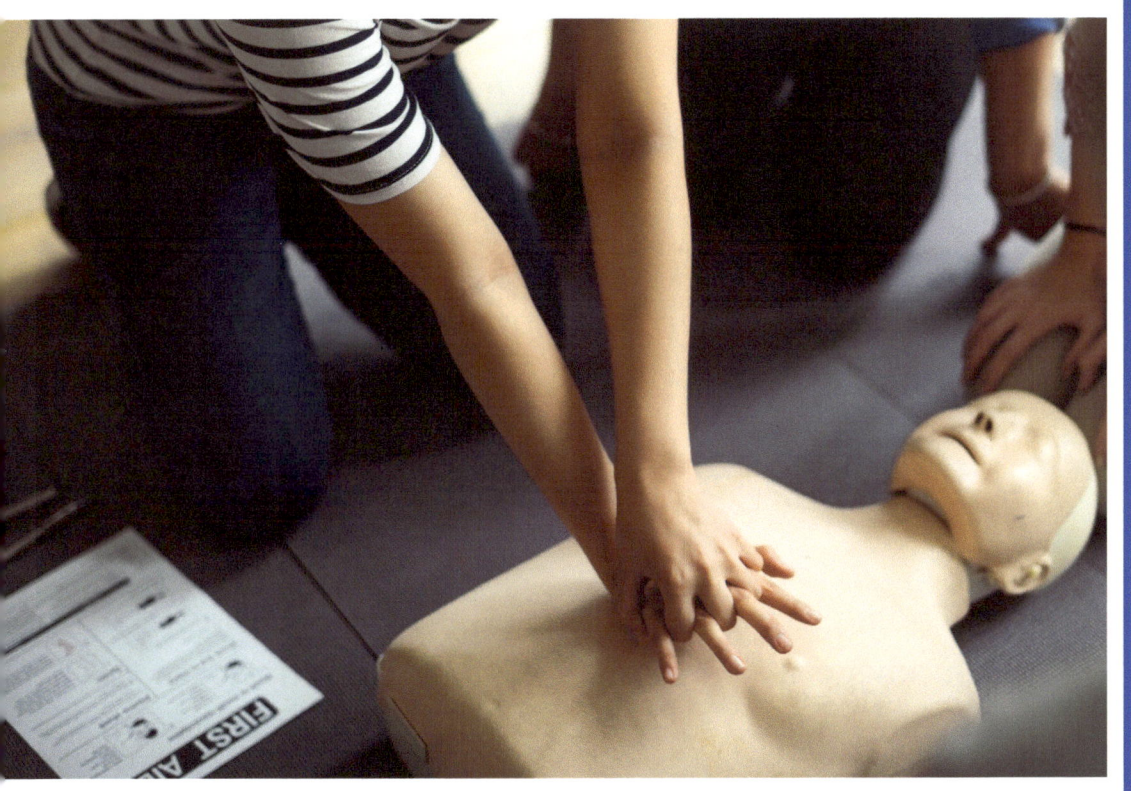

Bella Hope Smith

Suicide

Everything is getting too much, I'm finding life really tough. I feel like giving up, and just saying enough is enough.

How do I pick myself up when i'm feeling so depressed and low? I'm stuck in a vicious cycle, with no place to go.

I've lost all hope, and just don't know what to do. How can I change a negative to a positive point of view?

I am going to take the first step to change the way I feel; advice and support is what i'm going to seek. Knowing that I need some help, shows that I Am Strong not weak.

Bella Hope Smith

Homelessness

How would you feel being homeless and poor, with nothing to drink or eat?

Not being able to feel safe when your awake or trying to sleep.

Being out in all weathers from coldness and snow, to chucking it down with rain.

People just walking past you, not knowing your trauma, hurt and pain.

Nobody should be on the streets; cold, hungry and alone.

We need to work together so everyone can have food, comfort, security and a home.

Motor Neurone Disease

It's absolutely heartbreaking when someone is diagnosed with MND. Watching them deteriorate over time, is such a sad and devastating thing to see. A terrible neurological disease, that progresses effecting the spinal cord and brain. Causing such frustration, upset, misery and pain.

As degeneration happens, it can effect communication; causing a struggle or an inability to talk. A muscle wasting illness, that decreases mobility; stopping you from having the ability to stand up or walk.

Think about the family and friends, of someone who has MND and how they feel too. Trying to stay strong, but knowing the struggles they have to try and get through.

Change needs to happen, this awful disease has to come to a complete stop. We won't quit fighting, until MND comes to an end. We Will Come Out On Top. Research, funding and awareness is what we are striving for. We need to all work together to help find a cure.

All About Awareness

Autism

Autism is a neuro-developmental spectrum disorder, that effects behaviour and the way you act. It causes anxiety and a struggle to understand emotions, making it hard to socially interact. Sticking to routines is vital, as change can be hard to process. Breaking out of a familiar pattern, can cause feelings of worry, fear and stress.

Autism can cause a difficulty to form bonds, which may effect making friends and connecting. Being in social situations can be tough, which may cause overwhelm, confusion and may feel being around others upsetting. Sensory differences can happen also; like touch, taste, light and sound. Being in unfamiliar surroundings can be too much, causing them to sometimes retreat or shutdown.

There is no cure for Autism, but speech and behavioural therapies can help, along with creative outlets too. Helping express thoughts and feelings, in a more visionary and original point of view. The positive attributes to being Autistic, include being highly intelligent, very creative with a vivid imagination. Compassionate with a high attention to detail, and a strong sense of determination.

Bella Hope Smith

Grief

I'm heartbroken and stuck with this painful grief. I'm struggling to cope, I have no hope or belief.

My entire mind, body and soul is numb and in shock. I can't focus on anything; I want this sadness to stop.

Mixed feelings are whirling around me, I just can't take anymore. It's too hard to face life, when i'm feeling so vulnerable and raw.

I try to pretend that I am ok, by putting on a brave face. But I know grieving takes time, and happens at it's own pace.

I need some support to help me with this painful process; I need to talk about my feelings and cry. I wish I could talk to my loved ones, one last time; to say I love you and to properly say goodbye.

Bella Hope Smith

Tourette's

If I get really anxious and stressed. It causes my tics to get worse and progress.

I try so hard to stop them; but nothing seems to work. I can have physical tics that cause my body to twitch, jolt and jerk.

Though sometimes my tics are loud and verbal. What I say can come across as rude or hurtful.

But this is a neurological condition that I cannot stop. When I pent everything up, it feels like i'm going to pop.

Please don't judge me; I know that I stand out. I may make noises, behave differently and start moving about.

But when you see me ticking, please never forget. That I am the same as you, but i've got Tourette's.

All About Awareness

Body Dysmorphia

The way that I look and appear. Makes me so upset, that it brings me to tears.

I have so many defects, faults and flaws. I hate myself and don't want to go out anymore.

I'm fat, unattractive and can't bare to look at my face. It's so disgusting and ugly, it's an absolute disgrace.

I wish I was attractive, and had a body that looks good. With everything perfect and being as it should.

But I can't keep feeling like this, it's making me ill. I'm destroying myself. I am going to reach out for help, so I can get some support with my physical and mental health.

Bella Hope Smith

Cancer

I have noticed various symptoms and changes in my overall health. It's causing me to be anxious and worried, I haven't been feeling my normal self. It's so important to get checked, but i'm absolutely terrified. The stress and concern I feel, is knotting me up inside.

I am going to go in for some checks and extensive tests. My heart is beating so fast, that it wants to jump right out of my chest. I have got my results, and now I know what's wrong with me. The doctors gave me the bad news, that I have the Big C. When they said those words, I was stunned and frozen in fear. Pain and shock was in each and everyone of my tears. How do I get through this? I feel totally lost and in despair. What about all the treatment side effects? Will I lose my hair?

It is going to be a very tough and tiring journey; but my family and friends will be with me all the way. They give me so much love, strength and support, which gets me through each and everyday. The health professionals are really helping, and showing me how I can cope. I tell myself each day that I Am Going To Beat This. I have so much faith, belief and hope.

Bella Hope Smith

Anti-Discrimination

Do you think the world is in a bit of a state? With all the violence, abuse, discrimination and hate.

Are we doing enough to stop this once and for all? Have the rates of these terrible acts began to rise or fall?

If you commit these crimes, just reflect on what your doing. Think of all the lives that you will destroy and ruin.

All the pain and suffering from what you do or say. Can cause destruction to someone's life, in just a second or a day.

We need to show each other kindness, compassion and respect. Where inclusion, equality and fairness in life, is what we always get.

All About Awareness

Dyspraxia

Dyspraxia is a neurological co-ordination disorder; effecting movement, language and speech. It causes concentration and irritability problems, making new skills hard to teach.

Noise sensitivity, big crowds and bright lights can cause sensory overload. Too much stimulation can build up, creating a feeling like your mind is going to explode. Stuttering can happen too, making words hard to express. Causing frustration, upset and feelings of distress. Hand eye co-ordination is often poor, making it difficult to run, jump and even catch a ball. Balance and moving around can be hard, which can result in tripping, stumbling or a fall.

There is no cure to dyspraxia, but there are therapies that can help with relief. These include language, physical and occupational treatments, to help build confidence, self-esteem and belief. The positive attributes to dyspraxia include; being thoughtful, creative and very empathetic too. Great problem solvers with strong leadership skills, they work extremely hard in all that they do.

Bella Hope Smith

Alcoholism

Just one more drink I say to myself. But I can't just have one, I am now on my twelfth. I start with a couple of glasses, which turns into more and more. The drinking gets easier and easier, the more alcohol I pour.

When I think of not drinking, I get so down and low. Alcohol is like my best friend, it takes away my worries and pain all in one go. The temptation to keep drinking heavily, is too appealing for me. I can't go a day without it, not having alcohol is too hard to see.

How can I stop thinking of drinking? It's on my mind all day and night. I just can't stop this, I see no end in sight. My drinking is getting worse, and affecting all aspects of my life; causing me to spiral into depression. My personality has changed too; everyone says i'm short tempered and full of aggression.

I know I need to get this under control, and get back to the person I was before. I don't want to keep feeling so anxious, angry and alone anymore. My drinking has pushed others away, causing such hurt and friction. I know I need help now, to stop this crippling alcohol addiction.

Bella Hope Smith

Periods

Periods aren't just something that happens for upto a week. They can be extremely painful, very heavy and can sometimes leak.

Periods have many symptoms not only cramping and the amount that you bleed. You can have fever's, headache's, nausea and fatigue.

Many things can cause periods to differ, from unbalanced hormones to extreme stress. Women shouldn't feel like they can't ask for help if they are in a mess.

We need to talk about periods, without feeling any embarassment or shame. Getting awareness out about how periods affect women, is the biggest goal and aim.

All About Awareness

ADHD

ADHD is a neurodevelopmental disorder, that can cause a variety of symptoms including; a lack of focus, excessive talking and restlessness. Mood swings and emotional disruptions can happen, causing outbursts of anger and internal stress.

You may think children with ADHD are naughty, but it's the neurological condition causing this. Misbehaving can be just put down to bad behaviour, and a ADHD diagnosis can be missed.

Fidgeting and moving about, can make it hard for them to concentrate. ADHD can cause time management blindness, making them often delayed or late.

There are various treatments to help ADHD including; behavioural, cognitive, occupational and mindfulness therapies.

The positive attributes to ADHD include; being good at problem solving, great multi-taskers with a high level of creativity. They have lots of energy and enthusiasm, and can handle change and adaptability.

Bella Hope Smith

River Pollution

Have you seen the state of our rivers? They are an absolute disgrace. Full of pesticides, chemicals and hazardous waste.

Why have we let this happen? And go on for so long. Having things dumped in the rivers where they don't belong. Why are we treating the environment like this? Where the rivers are toxic, diseased and full of dead fish.

Seeing all this destruction and devastation, is such a sad and worrying sight. We are killing wildlife and their habitats, this is just not right. Stop putting paint, oils and fats down the sink. They cause more harm and problems than you think.

We need to stop littering and end single use plastics too. Disposing of your litter and re-cycling rubbish, is what you should do. We need to come together to help find a solution. To make all rivers clean, safe and free of pollution.

Bella Hope Smith

Anti-Knife Crime

What's going through your mind when you pick up a knife? Are you wanting to scare people, or take someone's life? Do you feel fearful and think you need one for protection? Do you want to go down the wrong path, living a life with no purpose or direction? How would you feel if you were the victim? Look at it from their side. Feeling extremely fearful, alarmed and absolutely terrified.

Your not only hurting someone else, your hurting their family and friends too. Think of all the pain, heartbreak and devastation that they will have to go through. Can you live with the guilt, regret and shame? Going through life knowing that you've caused so much trauma, suffering and pain.

How would your family and friends feel finding out what you have done? Will you feel ashamed? Or will you just hide away and run? Let's bring this to a complete stop. No one should be carrying or using a knife. Everyone should feel safe. Everyone should have a chance to live their life.

All About Awareness

Dyslexia

Words seem puzzling when I look at them; they just don't make sense. When somebody asks me to read or spell a word, I get very anxious and tense.

I get tough on myself when I struggle to read or write. I try so hard; why does it seem like a constant fight?

But I am not going to let it stop me, I know that for sure. I'm not going to be so hard on myself anymore.

I have so many gifts that I want to share with the world, including my fantastic problem solving skills and strong creative side.

When I see all the amazing talents that I have, I look at myself with pure admiration and pride.

Bella Hope Smith

Animal Cruelty

Why would you cause an animal to suffer in pain? Do you have no empathy, compassion or shame?

Animals shouldn't be hurt in anyway shape or form. Leaving them out in all weathers, where there not looked after or kept warm.

Why would you cause an animal to starve to death? Leaving them so weak and tired, that they are gasping for their last breath.

Animals shouldn't be scared of us, shaking and hiding in fear. Being in a constant state of stress and anxiety that's so severe.

They shouldn't be kept in cages, or tied up where they can't move and just be. How would you feel if you were left like this? Not being able to enjoy life and be free.

We cannot hurt, harm, abuse or neglect. All animals need to be treated with love, kindness, care and respect.

Bella Hope Smith

Loneliness

I'm so isolated. I am on my own. I don't have anyone to talk to. Nobody I can phone.

If I go out anywhere, no one stops to say how are you? Or even Hi. My loneliness is getting worse as the days pass by.

Everyday's the same through all the four seasons. I often wonder why my life is like this. What is the reason?

But I am going to try and go out at every opportunity. I'm going to join some clubs that are happening in my community.

Now a few months on I have made friends, that I meet or chat with on the phone. I'm not isolated anymore. I am not on my own.

All About Awareness

Skin Conditions

When I get upset, worried or stressed. My skin breaks out into a bit of a mess.

My hormones are out of balance and all over the place. My skin is particulary bad on my arms, back and face.

When I go out people look and stare; I just want to cover up and hide. It seems as if all my emotions are coming out from the inside.

My skin is unsightly, blotchy and sore. I just don't have confidence in myself anymore.

My irritated skin is telling me that something is out of sync. It could be a deficiency, genetics, anxiety or just the way that I think.

But my skin is part of me, I should embrace the way I look and feel. Loving my skin unconditionally is the only way I can heal.

Bella Hope Smith

Panic Attacks

I am ok. I am calm. I am on the right track. But something hits me hard, and puts my progress further back. One minute I am fine, and think everything is going good when clearly it's not. My heart is pounding fast, I can't breathe properly, and I am getting very hot.

What is happening? Why do I feel this way? It's starting to happen now every single day. It's affecting all aspects of my life, from my work, relationships and socialising. It's no wonder that I want to hide away; it's very uncomfortable and paralyzing.

I now realise that i'm having panic attacks, I have built up a lot of anxiety, fear and stress. I feel like i'm extremely stuck and my life has turned into a complete and utter mess.

I'm going to look into helping my panic attacks, through talking therapy, breathing exercises and relaxation. So I can control how I think and feel through every situation.

Bella Hope Smith

Domestic Abuse

I feel scared, I feel weak. I feel distressed, I can't sleep.

Is it something i've done to cause this? Am I the one to blame? If I tell anyone what's happening, I will feel such embarassment, upset and shame. Please get me out of this toxic and harmful place. I want to be somewhere that is full of love, peace and where I feel totally safe.

But I need some help, what shall I do? Will people believe me, and understand my point of view? This is something I need to call out and report. I need someone to listen to me, and give me comfort, compassion and support.

With useful information and someone to listen to my concerns and needs. I don't feel weak anymore. I Am Strong. I Am Freed. Let's make this a world where there is No violence, bullying or abuse. No one should be treated like this. There is absolutely No excuse.

All About Awareness

How To Write Your Own Awareness Poems

Choose a topic or topics that your truly passionate about.

Begin researching about the subject.

Start writing down words on how you feel about this topic. Putting your own thoughts and feelings into your poems, are key to creating a strong message.

Let your emotions pour onto paper, letting how you feel flow freely.

Remember your poems don't have to rhyme, just allow yourself to write with no pressure in trying to rhyme them.

Take your time in creating your powerful piece of poetry.

After you've finished your poem, you can share it with charities, organisations, put it on your social media, send it to a poetry competition, create a poetry blog, submit it to a magazine or even read it out on a podcast to get awareness out.

Finally make others Aware, Care & Share!

Bella Hope Smith

Self Awareness

I am going to show you a technique that you can use each day to check how you are feeling, using the words Aware, Care & Share.

Aware. Each day try and write down how you feel emotionally, physically and mentally. This will help you to become Aware of any changes you experience on any level. For example you could write today i'm feeling pain in my foot. Now write down all the feelings it's causing you to have, both emotionally and mentally and if you have any other symptoms in your body.

Care. After write down an action plan to take Care of yourself. For example you could write my foot is causing me discomfort, so I am going to get it checked with a health professional. I will do gentle exercises to ease the pain physically, do mindfulness to help me emotionally and say affirmations to help myself mentally.

Share. If you are struggling on any level either physically, mentally or emotionally, always know there are people to help you and listen. Share how you feel so your not keeping it to yourself, letting it build up with no outlet, causing a lot of internal stress.

All About Awareness

Thank you for reading my book. I hope you have enjoyed reading the powerful poems.

On the next few pages, are my other books that I have written and a bit about them. They are all available to buy online and from various book and gift shops.

Bella Hope Smith

Mighty Mind Mantra's For Men

This is a mindfulness book to help you express thoughts and feelings, through writing therapy, mindful exercises and mantra's to help change your mindset to think more positively.

I also teach you how to write powerful poems, your own mighty mantra's, relax through meditation, build an attitude of gratitude and much more.

All About Awareness

Rejuvenating Rhyming Affirmations

This is a unique book of my rhyming affirmations, crystal recommendations and healing meditations too.

I decided to rhyme all the affirmations, as rhyming gets the healing message into the mind quicker & easier, resulting in better overall outcomes. Rhyming helps with neurodiverse minds too.

Some of the affirmation topics in my book, are to help with

Grief. Sleep. Relaxation. Inner Child Healing. Overcoming Fear. Anxiety **and much more.**

Bella Hope Smith

Mystical, Spiritual, Poetical

This is a healing collection of spiritual poems, with pages to write gratitude lists, affirmations, prayers, poems & spiritual shapes to colour in for art therapy.

Some of the spiritual poem topics in the book include:

Crystals. Akashic Records. Tarot. Manifestation. Yoga. Chakra's and much more.

www.ingramcontent.com/pod-product-compliance
Lightning Source LLC
Chambersburg PA
CBHW041117070526
44584CB00002B/199